ice creams

hamlyn

ice creams

Notes

1 If using an ice cream machine, prepare the machine, and churn and freeze the ice cream following the manufacturer's instructions.

2 Both metric and imperial measures have been given in all recipes. Use one set of measurements only and not a mix of both.

3 Standard level spoon measurements are used in all recipes:
1 tablespoon = one 15 ml spoon
1 teaspoon = one 5 ml spoon

4 Milk should be full fat unless otherwise stated.

5 Eggs should be large unless otherwise stated. This book contains some dishes made with raw or lightly cooked eggs. It is prudent for more vulnerable people, such as pregnant and nursing mothers, invalids, the elderly, babies and young children, to avoid uncooked or lightly cooked dishes made with eggs.

6 Cooking times are based on stovetop cooking and not the total tabletop cooking unless otherwise stated.

7 This book includes dishes made with nuts and nut derivatives. It is advisable for those with known allergic reactions to nuts and nut derivatives and those who may be potentially vulnerable to these allergies, such as pregnant and nursing mothers, invalids, the elderly, babies and children, to avoid dishes made with nuts and nut oils. It is also prudent to check the labels of pre-prepared ingredients for the possible inclusion of nut derivatives.

First published in 2001
by Hamlyn
an imprint of Octopus Publishing Group Limited
2–4 Heron Quays, London, E14 4JP

ISBN 0 600 60331 8

A CIP catalogue record for this book is available from the British Library

Printed and bound in China

10 9 8 7 6 5 4 3 2 1

Contents

introduction

Ices and ice creams are a universal favourite, appealing to people of all ages all over the world – in cold countries as well as hot ones, and as popular in Russia as in the Tropics. Such is their appeal that they have been made out of almost every possible ingredient; ice creams made from tomatoes and asparagus were popular among the sophisticated between the two World Wars, and purple yam ice cream can be bought in the Philippines today.

Ice and Ice Creams in History

Chilled foods and wines are as old as civilization, for the histories of ice for storage and ices to eat are inextricably bound together. To have been in the happy position of being able to serve chilled food and ice to guests in hot weather must have been one of the world's first status symbols. The Mesopotamians, the Chinese and the ancient Greeks and Romans all conserved snow and winter ice for use in the summer, and the first ice houses came into existence in about 2000 BC. In the 16th century, the Mughal emperors sent relays of horsemen to bring back ice and snow from the Hindu Kush for the fruit-flavoured sorbets enjoyed by the rich and powerful in Delhi. In the 17th century, in Allahabad in Bengal, there was a four-acre site used for ice-making when the night-time temperatures were low enough and, at the same time, travellers in Persia seeing the ice houses in the great salt desert commented on the wonders of ice for preservation.

Cream ices originated in 17th-century Italy, still the home of some of the best ice cream in the world, and in May 1671 "one plate of Ice Cream" was served at Windsor Castle, the first recorded mention of a cream ice in England. In 1751, Mrs Hannah Glasse included a recipe for raspberry ice cream in an edition of her book *The Art of Cookery Made Plain and Easy*, and in Frederic Nutt's *Complete Confectioner*, published in 1789, there were no fewer than 31 ice creams, including a selection of fruit flavours and chocolate, coffee and pistachio – in fact, very much a selection that would be popular today. During the 18th century, water ices were preferred in France, Italy and other parts of continental Europe, while the British and the Americans opted for cream ices.

Ice houses were slow to gain acceptance in Britain, but after the restoration of Charles II, who had an ice house built in St James's Park, they became popular and by the middle of the 18th century, every country estate of any consequence, with its own lake, had an ice house. They were generally built of brick or stone and shaped like a well, with sloping sides about 4–5 metres (12–15 feet) deep and a soakaway at the bottom, and topped by a domed roof. They were insulated by layers of earth, surrounded by trees and approached through a long tunnel, closed off by a series of doors. A vent in the roof helped to ensure dryness, for a damp atmosphere encouraged the ice to melt. The ice was cut from the lake, and carried or slid to the ice house and layered with straw for insulation.

During the 19th century, top-quality ice was exported from New England to Britain and the Caribbean (the most famous company was the Wenham Lake Ice Co. of Massachusetts) and Norway also supplied the UK, particularly ports in the north. Shipping ice was a hazardous business, for one-fifth of the cargo could melt on the voyage from the USA to Britain.

Ice cream has always been popular in the USA. George Washington's household goods included a "cream machine for making ice", while Dolley Madison, society hostess and wife of James Madison, the 4th president of the USA, served an ice cream topped with strawberries at their second inaugural ball. Captain Marryat, author of *The*

Children of the New Forest, who travelled extensively in the USA in 1837, recorded with surprise that "ice creams are universal and very cheap". In the early days, ice cream making required considerable strength and stamina on the part of the cook, for lengthy hand beating was required to make the ice cream mixture smooth as it froze. However, in the 1840s, Nancy Johnson, an American, invented the hand-cranked freezer, but sadly, she failed to patent her invention.

Two more American innovations came next. In 1874 the first ice cream soda (made of milk, flavoured syrup and a scoop of ice cream) made its appearance at the semicentennial of the Franklin Institute in Philadelphia, then, in 1881, an ice cream parlour in Two Rivers, Michigan, served the first ice cream sundae, with a topping of chocolate syrup. This new delicacy is said to have earned its name because first of all it was for sale only as a Sunday treat.

Cornets appeared independently on both sides of the Atlantic around the turn of the 20th century. Mrs Agnes Marshall, proprietor of Marshall's School of Cookery in London, W1, and the author of several best-selling cookery books, was particularly interested in ice cream. In *Fancy Ices*, published in 1894, there are recipes, with illustrations, for cornets, which were filled with ices, piled on a serving dish and served as a dinner party dessert, to be eaten with a spoon and fork. American cornets were first seen at the St Louis World's Fair in 1904, a fortuitous improvisation when the supply of ice cream dishes ran out.

The first domestic refrigerators appeared just before World War 1, but in Britain, they remained out of most people's reach until the 1950s. In 1939 only one house in 50 boasted a refrigerator; instead, they had ice boxes, wooden containers lined with zinc and usually insulated with felt, which had a compartment for blocks of ice. This was sold from door to door by itinerant salesmen with horse-drawn carts. The arrival of the domestic freezer in the 1960s has made ice cream making comparatively easy, while recent developments in the form of sophisticated electric home ice cream makers have made it simplicity itself.

Making Ices

Iced desserts have the enormous advantage for the busy hostess in that they must be made in advance and that, on the whole, they don't require very much of the cook's time, merely a lengthy wait while the mixture freezes. Basically, there are only two types of ice. Firstly, sorbets, which include water ices and granitas, and are generally light and refreshing. Secondly, there are cream ices, which should be smooth, rich, and sumptuous.

When making iced desserts, it helps to know a little about the freezing process. Without any additions, a fruit purée, the basis of many ices, would freeze to the solid consistency of an ice lolly, but when other ingredients, such as sugar, cream, gelatine, eggs, alcohol and air, are added to the purée they prevent it from freezing quite so hard. In general, the higher the ratio of cream to the basic flavouring, the less beating is necessary. This means that if an ice contains a high proportion of water (a sorbet made with fruit juice, for example), then ice crystals will form easily and, for a smooth finish, the ice will need a considerable amount of beating and stirring. The quantity of sugar in a recipe is vital to both ice creams and sorbets. Too much sugar and the ice won't freeze properly; not enough and it will be hard to scoop.

Alcohol also retards freezing. Ices with a little alcohol are soft to scoop, but ices with too much may not freeze hard enough. Instead of risking a slushy finish, you can drizzle a little more liqueur or spirit over the ice at the table.

Varied textures can make an ice cream more interesting. Rocky Road (see page 24) includes pieces of chocolate, marshmallows and raisins. It is similar to the Russian *plombir*, a rich ice cream with ground almonds, raisins and crystallized fruit – a sort of tutti-frutti. Plain ice cream flavoured with toasted breadcrumbs, which give it a nutty flavour, was an old English favourite, while large pieces of crushed meringue give vanilla ice cream an unusual finish.

Granitas These are usually made with fruit juice or coffee, sugar and, sometimes, alcohol and served ice cold in tall glasses, sometimes layered with cream, to be eaten with a spoon. Unlike sorbets and ice creams, they have a grainy texture.

Sorbets and Water Ices Like granitas, these have a sugar syrup base, but often include beaten egg whites to lighten the mixture and give a smoother texture. The word sorbet (and also sherbet) comes from the Arabic *shariba*, meaning a drink. Sorbets are often served in sundae glasses or in tall glasses like granitas.

Cream Ices These contain fats, usually in the form of cream and/or egg custard. Some cream ices are frozen to the correct consistency without further beatings, but although custard-based ice creams may include whipped cream, the custard base does not have sufficient air to prevent ice crystals from forming, so these ices must be beaten during freezing to get rid of any graininess which would otherwise spoil the texture of the finished dish.This only applies if you are making the ice cream by hand. If an ice cream maker is being used the machine will do the beating whilst it is churning and freezing.

Sugar Boiling

Sugar syrups are the basis of many sorbets and ice creams. The most accurate way to identify which of the different stages the syrup has reached during cooking is to use a sugar thermometer. Listed below are the temperatures for the different stages of sugar boiling that have been used in this book, together with quick, alternative tests which are easy to use if you do not have a sugar thermometer.

Thread Stage (107°C/225°F)
Using a small spoon remove a little of the syrup and let it fall from the spoon on to a dish. The syrup should form a fine thin thread.

Soft Ball (113–118°C/235–245°F)
Drop a small amount of the syrup into iced water. Mould the sticky syrup into a soft ball with the fingers. Remove the ball from the water. It should immediately lose its shape.

Hard Ball (120–130°C/248–266°F)
Drop a little syrup into iced water then mould it into a ball with your fingers. Remove the ball from the water. It should feel resistant to the fingers and still quite sticky.

Light Caramel (160–177°C/320–350°F)
Using a small spoon remove a little of the syrup and pour it on to a white saucer. The syrup should be a light golden brown colour. Do not allow it to reach the final stage of dark caramel, when it loses its sweetness.

Ice Cream Dishes

A sorbet or ice cream can be served on its own, with a simple decoration (see page 11), or used as the base for a more complicated dish. Listed below are some famous composite ice cream dishes.

Baked Alaska – A sponge cake topped with ice cream, surrounded by meringue and baked for 3–4 minutes at a high heat to cook the meringue. The meringue insulates the ice cream from the heat, so it is essential that there are no gaps in the meringue covering. It is also known as the **Surprise Omelette** or **Norwegian Omelette**.

Banana Split – A banana split lengthwise, with vanilla ice cream along its length, and drizzled with hot fudge sauce and topped with whipped cream, chopped nuts, and a Maraschino cherry.

Ice Cream Bombe – Layers of ice cream are frozen one at a time in a spherical mould.

Ice Cream Charlotte – A charlotte mould is lined with sponge fingers and filled with ice cream. It is often lavishly decorated with whipped cream.

Peach Melba – A concoction of poached peaches with vanilla ice cream, topped with raspberry sauce, this dish was created by the great chef Escoffier for the Australian opera singer, Dame Nellie Melba, in the 1880s.

Decorating Sorbets & Ice Creams

Ice creams and sorbets lend themselves to a huge range of decorations. Caramelized fruit goes well with any flavour ice cream that the fruit complements. For instance serve **caramelized cherries** with Cherry Chocolate Ice Cream (see page 19).

To make the caramelized cherries pour ½ cup of water into a heavy saucepan and add ¾ cup of caster sugar. Heat gently until the sugar has dissolved. Increase the heat and cook rapidly until the syrup begins to caramelize and is golden brown. The temperature will register 160–177° (320–350°F) on a sugar thermometer – light caramel stage (see page 10) – then remove from the heat. Dip the cherries into the caramel and place on a sheet of lightly oiled foil and leave to cool. Dip a fork into the caramel, then shake quickly over the cherries to create a nest effect.

Citrus fruit ices look good with slices or twists of orange, lemon, or lime, or a **fruit syrup**.

To make the fruit syrup pour 2 tablespoons of water into a heavy saucepan and add 2 tablespoons of honey and 50 g (2 oz) of fruit. Heat until

boiling then pour through a wire mesh strainer. Discard the fruit and pour the syrup over the ice cream.

Candied peel works very well with fruit sorbets or ice creams.

To make the candied peel pour ¼ cup of water in a heavy saucepan and add ½ cup of caster sugar. Add finely chopped peel and heat gently until the sugar has dissolved and it has turned into a light syrup. Remove from the heat, drain the peel, and coat with a little superfine sugar.

Herbs, especially mint, lemon balm and borage, and sprigs of red-, white- or blackcurrants look good with many ices, as do edible flowers and **frosted leaves, flowers and little fruits**, such as whole grapes or redcurrant sprigs. These are easy to prepare.

To make the frosted fruit coat the chosen flower or fruit in lightly beaten egg white, then sprinkle caster sugar over to cover. Set aside to dry on a wire rack or wax paper. Drying takes about 2 hours.

Chocolate shavings or grated chocolate go well with chocolate, coffee and vanilla ice creams, while whipped cream adds a luscious finishing touch to most creamy ices. Nuts are another good topping, while crisp biscuits, such as fan wafers, langues de chat and amaretti, make a crunchy contrast to the smoothness of ice cream. **Pralines** are a perfect accompaniment to ices such

as Honeyed Banana Ice Cream with Nuts (see page 40).

To make the pralines pour ¼ cup of water into a heavy saucepan and add ¾ cup of caster sugar and 2 tablespoons of golden syrup. Simmer gently until the sugar has dissolved to make a caramel syrup. Place 1¼ cups of toasted almonds on a lightly oiled piece of foil and pour the syrup over. Let set for 1 hour. Once set, break up into irregular pieces and serve with the ice cream.

A hot sauce, such as fudge or chocolate, makes another good contrast with the coldness of ice cream and can help soften an ice which has set too hard or has too grainy a texture. It is worth buying an ice-cream scoop rather than serving sorbets and ice creams with a spoon – the finished shape looks more attractive and professional.

Storing Ices

To keep them in the freezer, pack ice creams and sorbets in rigid polythene boxes with tight-fitting lids, and transfer them to the refrigerator about 30 minutes before you want to serve them. The longer an ice has been stored, the more softening time it will need. Ice creams can be stored in the freezer for about 3 months and sorbets for 1–2 months. Granitas cannot be stored in the freezer, as they will turn into a solid mass.

strawberry ice cream

500 g (1 lb) strawberries, hulled

4 tablespoons fresh orange juice

175 g (6 oz) caster sugar

450 ml (¾ pint) whipping cream

to decorate:

wild strawberries

strawberry syrup (see page 11)

1 Finely mash the strawberries and mix with the orange juice to form a smooth purée. Stir in the sugar.*

2 Whip the cream until it forms soft peaks and fold into the purée. Pour the mixture into a 1 kg (2 lb) loaf tin. Freeze for 1½ hours or until partly frozen.

3 Turn the mixture into a bowl, break it up with a fork and then whisk until smooth. Return the mixture to the loaf tin and freeze for at least 5 hours until completely frozen.

4 Transfer to the refrigerator 30 minutes before serving, to soften. Decorate with wild strawberries and strawberry syrup.

* *If using an ice cream machine follow the recipe until the end of step **1**. Place the mixture in the machine and add the cream. Churn and freeze following the manufacturer's instructions (see note 1, on page 4). Serve with strawberries.*

Serves 6
Preparation time: **15 minutes, plus freezing**

blackberry ice cream

500 g (1 lb) blackberries

2 tablespoons caster sugar

125 ml (4 fl oz) water

50 g (2 oz) granulated sugar

3 egg yolks

450 ml (¾ pint) single cream

2 tablespoons icing sugar, sifted

2 tablespoons rosewater

1 Put the blackberries into a pan with the caster sugar, stir well and simmer over a low heat for 10 minutes or until tender. Rub through a sieve and leave to cool.

2 Put the water and granulated sugar into a pan and heat gently, stirring until the sugar has dissolved. Increase the heat and boil steadily until the syrup reaches a temperature of 107°C/225°F on a sugar thermometer – thread stage (see page 10). Leave the syrup to cool.

3 Put the egg yolks in a bowl and pour the syrup over, whisking until the mixture is thick and mousse-like.

4 Mix the cream with the fruit purée, icing sugar and rosewater and fold into the mousse.* Turn into a freezer container, cover and freeze.

5 Transfer to the refrigerator about 30 minutes before serving to soften. Scoop into chilled glasses and serve.

* *If using an ice cream machine follow the recipe until mid way through step **4**. Turn the mixture into the machine and churn and freeze.*

Serves 8
Preparation time: **10 minutes, plus cooling and freezing**
Cooking time: **about 20 minutes**

mango ice cream

300 ml (½ pint) water

100 g (4 oz) caster sugar

1 ripe mango, peeled, halved and stoned

2 tablespoons lemon juice

150 ml (5 fl oz) double or whipping cream

1 Put the water and sugar into a heavy-based saucepan and heat gently, stirring, until the sugar has dissolved. Increase the heat and boil steadily until the syrup reaches a temperature of 107°C/225°F on a sugar thermometer – thread stage (see page 10). Remove from the heat and leave to cool.

2 Purée the mango flesh in a food processor or blender with the lemon juice. Then stir the purée into the syrup. *

3 Place the mixture into a freezer container and freeze for about 1½ hours until mushy.

4 Beat the cream until it forms soft peaks. Fold into the frozen mango mixture and freeze. Beat the mixture twice, at hourly intervals. Cover, seal and freeze.

5 Scoop the ice cream into serving dishes and serve with crisp wafers, if liked.

* *If using an ice cream machine follow recipe until the end of step **2**. Pour the mixture into the machine, add the cream and churn and freeze. Follow the serving suggestion in step **5**.*

Serves 4–6
Preparation time: **20 minutes, plus cooling and freezing**
Cooking time: **about 8 minutes**

st clements ice cream

3 eggs, separated

175 g (6 oz) caster sugar

grated rind and juice of 1 lemon

grated rind and juice of 1 orange

300 ml (½ pint) double or whipping cream

1 Whisk together the egg yolks, half of the sugar and the lemon and orange rinds in a heatproof bowl until thick and creamy. Strain the orange and lemon juice into saucepan and heat gently. Place the egg mixture in the heatproof bowl over simmering water and gradually whisk in the hot fruit juice. Whisk steadily until creamy. Take off the heat and continue whisking until cool.

2 Whisk the egg whites until stiff, then whisk in the remaining sugar. Fold into the egg mixture with the cream.*

3 Turn the mixture into a rigid freezer-proof container. Cover, seal and freeze until firm.

4 Scoop into chilled glasses and serve with wafer biscuits, if liked.

*If using an ice cream machine follow recipe until the end of step 2. Pour the mixture into the machine, and churn and freeze. Follow the serving suggestion in step 4.

Serves 6–8
Preparation time: **20 minutes, plus freezing**
Cooking time: **5 minutes**

peach ice cream

4 large, ripe peaches, total weight about 750 g (1½ lb), skinned

50 g (2 oz) icing sugar

1 tablespoon lemon juice

2 tablespoons white wine

2 teaspoons gelatine

4 egg yolks

300 ml (½ pint) double cream

waffle cones dipped in melted chocolate and pistachios, to serve

1 Purée the peach flesh with the sugar in a blender or food processor. Mix together the lemon juice and wine in a small bowl and sprinkle on the gelatine.

2 Transfer the peach purée to a large heatproof bowl. Beat in the egg yolks. Place the bowl over a pan of gently simmering water and stir until it thickens.

3 Put the bowl of gelatine mixture into a shallow pan of hot water and leave until it dissolves. Stir the gelatine into the peach mixture and leave to cool. *

4 Whip the cream until it forms soft peaks, then fold it into the peach mixture.

5 Transfer it to a freezer container, cover and freeze until firm, beating twice at hourly intervals. Serve with waffle cones dipped in melted plain chocolate and crushed pistachio nuts.

* *If using an ice cream machine follow recipe until end of step 3. Pour the mixture into the machine, add the cream and churn and freeze. Follow the serving suggestion at the end of step 5.*

Serves 6–8
Preparation time: **20 minutes, plus cooling and freezing**
Cooking time: **15 minutes**

crystallized ginger ice cream

125 ml (4 fl oz) water

75 g (3 oz) granulated sugar

3 egg yolks

300 ml (½ pint) double cream

75 g (3 oz) stem ginger, finely chopped

1 Place the water and sugar in a saucepan and heat gently, stirring, until the sugar has dissolved. Increase the heat and boil steadily until the syrup reaches a temperature of 107°C/225°F on a sugar thermometer – thread stage (see page 10). Leave the syrup to cool.

2 Put the egg yolks into a bowl and pour the syrup over, whisking until the mixture is thick and mousse-like. Whip the cream until it stands in soft peaks, then fold in the ginger, followed by the egg mixture. *

3 Turn into a freezer container, cover and freeze until firm. Transfer the ice cream to the refrigerator 30 minutes before serving to soften.

* *If using an ice cream machine follow the recipe until the end of step 2, taking care not to over-whip the cream. Pour the mixture into the machine and churn and freeze .*

Serves 4–6
Preparation time: **20 minutes, plus cooling and freezing**
Cooking time: **10 minutes**

rum & raisin ice cream

2 tablespoons rum

125 g (4 oz) raisins

75 g (3 oz) sugar

125 ml (4 fl oz) water

3 egg yolks

1 teaspoon vanilla essence

450 ml (¾ pint) double cream

1 Put the rum into a small bowl, add the raisins and leave to macerate for 4 hours.

2 Meanwhile, put the sugar and water into a small heavy-based saucepan and stir occasionally over a low heat until the sugar has dissolved. Increase the heat and boil rapidly for 5 minutes.

3 Place the egg yolks and vanilla essence in a bowl and whip until light and creamy. Beating constantly, slowly pour the hot syrup on to the egg yolk mixture. * Leave to cool then add the marinated raisins.

4 Whip the cream until just stiff then fold into the egg and raisin mixture.

5 Pour into a rigid shallow container, cover and place in the freezer. Remove the ice cream after 1 hour, turn into a bowl and beat well. Return it to the container and freeze again for 1 hour.

6 Remove the ice cream, turn it into a bowl and beat again, then return it to the container and freeze again.

7 To serve, transfer the ice cream to the refrigerator for about 30 minutes before serving to soften.

* If using an ice cream machine follow the recipe until mid way through step 3. Pour the egg mixture into the machine, add the cream and churn and freeze. Once frozen mix in the marinated raisins.

Serves 6
Preparation time: **20 minutes, plus macerating, cooling and freezing**
Cooking time: **10 minutes**

cherry chocolate ice cream

425 g (14 oz) can pitted black cherries in syrup

1 tablespoon cornflour

125 g (4 oz) luxury double chocolate cookies

2 Cadbury's Flakes

200 g (7 oz) plain chocolate, broken into pieces

450 ml (¾ pint) double cream

2 tablespoons icing sugar

2 teaspoons vanilla essence

200 g (7 oz) Greek yogurt

caramelized cherries (see page 11), to decorate (optional)

1 Drain the cherries, reserving the syrup. Blend a little of the syrup with the cornflour in a small saucepan. Stir in the remaining syrup and bring to the boil, stirring until thickened. Cook gently for 1 minute. Remove the pan from the heat, stir in the cherries and leave to cool.

2 Put the chocolate cookies into a plastic bag and tap them gently with a rolling pin to break them into small pieces. Crumble the Flakes into chunky pieces.

3 Melt the plain chocolate with 75 ml (3 fl oz) of the cream in a heatproof bowl set over a pan of simmering water. Stir gently until smooth then leave to cool slightly.

4 Whip the remaining cream in a bowl with the icing sugar, vanilla essence and yogurt until the cream just starts to hold its shape. Stir in half the plain chocolate mixture. Gently fold in the pieces of chocolate cookie and Flake.

5 Place spoonfuls of the remaining chocolate mixture and the cherries in syrup over the cream mixture. Using a large metal spoon, gently fold all the ingredients together until combined, but still with a slightly rippled effect. Turn into a freezer container and freeze for at least 4 hours.

6 Transfer the ice cream to the refrigerator about 30 minutes before serving to soften. Spoon into glasses and decorate with caramelized cherries, if liked.

* *Please note that this ice cream should not be made in an ice cream machine.*

Serves 6–8
Preparation time: **20 minutes, plus cooling and freezing**
Cooking time: **4–5 minutes**

cherry almond ice cream

150 ml (¼ pint) milk

50 g (2 oz) ground almonds

1 egg and 1 extra yolk

75 g (3 oz) caster sugar

2–3 drops almond essence

500 g (1 lb) red cherries, pitted, or 500 g (1lb) cherry compôte

25 g (1 oz) slivered almonds

150 ml (¼ pint) double cream

1 Pour the milk into a small saucepan and stir in the ground almonds. Bring to the boil, then set aside.

2 Put the egg and the extra yolk into a heatproof bowl with the sugar and beat until pale and thick. Pour on the milk and almond mixture. Place the bowl over a pan of gently simmering water and stir until thick. Stir in the almond essence and leave to cool.

3 Put the cherries into a food processor or blender and whizz to a purée, then stir them into the custard.

4 Toss the slivered almonds in a heavy pan over a low heat to toast them. Leave to cool. *

5 Whip the cream until it forms soft peaks. Fold the whipped cream into the cherry mixture. Transfer the mixture to a freezer container, cover and freeze until firm, beating twice at hourly intervals. Stir the slivered almonds into the mixture at the last beating. Serve the ice cream in individual glasses.

* If using an ice cream machine follow the recipe until the end of step 4. Pour the cherry mixture into the machine, add the cream and churn and freeze. Once frozen fold through the slivered almonds. Follow the serving suggestion at the end of step 5.

Serves 6
Preparation time: **20 minutes, plus cooling and freezing**
Cooking time: **20 minutes**

old-fashioned vanilla ice cream

300 ml (½ pint) single cream

1 vanilla pod

4 egg yolks

50 g (2 oz) caster sugar

300 ml (½ pint) double or whipping cream

to serve:

redcurrants coated in icing sugar (optional)

hot caramel sauce (see below)

1 Put the single cream and vanilla pod into a heavy-based saucepan, set over a low heat and bring to just below boiling point. Remove from the heat and leave to infuse.

2 Meanwhile, put the egg yolks and sugar into a heatproof bowl and set over a pan of gently simmering water. Stir with a wooden spoon until thick and creamy, then gradually stir in the scalded single cream, discarding the vanilla pod. Continue stirring for 15 minutes until the custard coats the back of the spoon. Remove the bowl from the heat and leave to cool. *

3 Pour the vanilla mixture into a freezer container, cover and transfer to the freezer for about 45 minutes or until slushy. Whip the cream until it just holds its shape. Remove the vanilla mixture from the freezer, beat

thoroughly, then fold in the cream. Return the mixture to the container, cover and freeze for a further 45 minutes, then beat again until smooth.

4 Freeze the ice cream for at least 1–2 hours. Transfer to the refrigerator for about 30 minutes to soften slightly before serving. Decorate with redcurrants coated in icing sugar and hot caramel sauce.

* *If using an ice cream machine follow the recipe until the end of step 2. Pour the vanilla mixture into the machine, add the cream and churn and freeze. Follow the serving suggestion at the end of step 4.*

Serves 6
Preparation time: **10 minutes, plus cooling and freezing**
Cooking time: **25 minutes**

hot caramel sauce

200 ml (7 fl oz) water

75 g (3 oz) caster sugar

juice of ½ lemon

1 Pour 150 ml (¼ pint) of the water into a heavy-based saucepan and add the sugar. Heat gently until the sugar has dissolved. Increase the heat and cook rapidly until the syrup begins to caramelize. The temperature will register 177°C/350°F on a sugar thermometer – caramel stage (see page 10).

2 Remove from the heat and gradually stir in the remaining water with the lemon juice. Leave to cool, then gently reheat the sauce before serving.

Makes 300 ml (½ pint)
Preparation time: **10 minutes**
Cooking time: **20 minutes**

rocky road ice cream

1 litre (1¾ pints) chocolate chip ice cream (see page 34)

2 Crunchie bars

3 standard packets white chocolate buttons

75 g (3 oz) mini marshmallows

50 g (2 oz) raisins

to serve:

chocolate sauce (see page 28)

chocolate shavings

Plain ice creams can be enhanced using different ingredients, such as raisins, marshmallows and chocolate chips, as in this classic variation on chocolate ice cream.

1 Transfer the ice cream to the refrigerator for 30–60 minutes to let it soften slightly.

2 Meanwhile, chop the Crunchie bars into small irregular pieces, reserving all the crumbs. Lightly crush the chocolate buttons while they are still in their packets to break them into slightly smaller pieces. Mix together the Crunchie and white chocolate button pieces, marshmallows and raisins.

3 Turn the ice cream into a bowl and break it up with a spoon. Add the remaining ingredients to the bowl and mix until dispersed throughout the ice cream. Transfer to a freezer container, cover and place in the freezer for several hours or overnight. Serve spooned into glasses.

* *Please note that there is no need to make this ice cream in an ice cream machine.*

Serves 6
Preparation time: **10 minutes, plus freezing**

coconut ice cream

350 ml (12 fl oz) milk

75 g (3 oz) desiccated coconut

350 ml (12 fl oz) single cream

2 eggs

2 egg yolks

125 g (4 oz) sugar

¼ teaspoon salt

1 Put the milk, coconut and cream into a heavy-based pan and bring very slowly to just below boiling point – about 15–20 minutes. Push through a fine sieve, pressing out as much of the coconut liquid as possible. Discard the coconut from the sieve.

2 Put the eggs and egg yolks, sugar and salt into a heatproof bowl and beat until thick and mousse-like. Place the bowl over a pan of simmering water, stir in some of the coconut cream mixture, then add the remainder and cook until the mixture is thick enough to coat the back of a spoon. Leave to cool. *

3 Pour into a shallow freezer container, cover and freeze until slushy. Beat to break up the ice crystals, return to the freezer container and freeze for about 2–3 hours until firm.

4 Transfer the ice cream to the refrigerator about 30 minutes before serving to soften slightly.

***** *If using an ice cream machine follow the recipe until the end of step **2**. Pour the cooled mixture into the machine and churn and freeze.*

Makes about 900 ml (1½ pints)
Preparation time: **15 minutes, plus freezing**
Cooking time: **15–20 minutes**

greengage plum ice cream

500 g (1 lb) greengage plums

1 tablespoon lemon juice

75 g (3 oz) soft brown sugar

1 whole egg, separated, and
1 extra yolk

150 ml (¼ pint) double cream

waffle wafers, to serve (optional)

1 Put the greengage plums in a saucepan with the lemon juice, cover and simmer gently until they are very soft. Press the greengage plums through a sieve into a heatproof bowl.

2 Stir the sugar into the greengage pulp, then stir in the egg yolks. Place the bowl over a pan of gently simmering water and stir until the mixture thickens. Remove from the heat and set aside to cool, then chill in the refrigerator for 1 hour. *

3 Whip the cream until it forms soft peaks, then fold it into the greengage mixture.

4 Transfer the mixture to a freezer container, cover and freeze for about 1 hour until firm round the edges.

5 Beat the egg white until stiff. Beat the greengage mixture with a fork to combine the frozen and partially frozen areas. Fold in the egg white, return to the freezer and freeze until firm.

6 Serve the ice cream with waffle wafers if liked.

* If using an ice cream machine follow the recipe until the end of step 2. Pour the mixture into the machine, add the cream and churn and freeze until it is half frozen. Whip the egg whites until they form soft peaks and add to the half-frozen mixture. Continue to freeze until completely frozen. Follow the serving suggestion in step 6.

Serves 4
Preparation time: **20 minutes, plus cooling and freezing**
Cooking time: **20 minutes**

chocolate ice cream

300 ml (½ pint) double cream

2 tablespoons milk

50 g (2 oz) icing sugar, sifted

½ teaspoon vanilla essence

125 g (4 oz) good-quality plain chocolate, broken into pieces

2 tablespoons single cream

chocolate sauce, to serve (optional)

1 Put the double cream and milk into a bowl and whisk until just stiff. Stir in the icing sugar and vanilla essence. Pour the mixture into a shallow freezer container and freeze for 30 minutes or until the ice cream begins to set around the edges.

2 Place the chocolate in a heatproof bowl with the single cream, set over a pan of gently simmering water and stir gently with a wooden spoon until melted and smooth. Set aside to cool.

3 Remove the ice cream from the freezer and spoon into a bowl. Add the melted chocolate and quickly stir it through the ice cream with a fork. Return the ice cream to the freezer container, cover and freeze until set.

4 Transfer the ice cream to the refrigerator 30 minutes before serving, to soften slightly. Serve with chocolate sauce if liked.

* *Please note that this ice cream cannot be made in an ice cream machine.*

Tip:
If the mixture splits at step **2**, add 2 tablespoons of water and stir well.

Serves 4
Preparation time: **20 minutes, plus cooling and freezing**
Cooking time: **10 minutes**

chocolate sauce

150ml (¼ pint) water

3 tablespoons caster sugar

150g (5 oz) dark plain chocolate

1 Gently heat all the ingredients in a saucepan, stirring, until melted. Serve the sauce immediately.

Makes about ½ pint
Preparation time: **5 minutes**

mint chocolate chip ice cream

2 egg whites

125 g (4 oz) caster sugar

400 g (13 oz) can evaporated milk, chilled

4 drops green food colouring

½ teaspoon peppermint essence

75 g (3 oz) plain chocolate, finely chopped

1 Whisk the egg whites until stiff, then gradually whisk in the sugar. Place the evaporated milk in a bowl with the food colouring and peppermint essence and whisk until thick, then fold into the meringue mixture with the chocolate. *

2 Turn into a freezer container, cover and freeze for 2 hours. Remove from the freezer and stir vigorously. Re-freeze until firm.

3 Transfer the ice cream to the refrigerator 30 minutes before serving to soften. Scoop into chilled dishes.

* *If using an ice cream machine follow the recipe until the end of step 1. Place the mixture in the machine and churn and freeze.*

Serves 8
Preparation time: **20 minutes, plus freezing**

hot fudge sauce

50 g (2 oz) dark chocolate, broken into small pieces

2 tablespoons golden syrup

100 g (4 oz) caster sugar

1 tablespoon cocoa

5 tablespoons hot water

1 tablespoon cold water

1 Put the chocolate in a heavy-based saucepan with the golden syrup, sugar, cocoa and hot water. Stir over a gentle heat until melted.

2 Increase the heat and cook rapidly, without stirring, until the soft ball stage is reached (see page 10). Remove from the heat and gently stir in the butter and cold water.

Makes: 175 ml (6 fl oz)
Preparation time: **5 mintues**
Cooking time: **about 10 minutes**

chocolate & mascarpone ice cream with coffee syrup

250 g (8 oz) caster sugar

375 ml (13 fl oz) water

300 g (10 oz) plain chocolate, finely chopped

75 g (3 oz) chocolate chips

250 g (8 oz) mascarpone cheese

2 tablespoons lemon juice

300 ml (½ pint) whipping cream

4 tablespoons coffee liqueur

1 Put 25 g (1 oz) of the sugar into a heavy-based saucepan with 150 ml (¼ pint) of the water. Heat gently until the sugar dissolves, then bring to the boil and boil rapidly for 3 minutes. Transfer the syrup to a bowl, stir in the chopped chocolate and leave until melted. (If the syrup cools before the chocolate has melted, heat it briefly in the microwave.)

2 Reserve 25 g (1 oz) of the chocolate chips. Finely chop or crush the remainder. Beat the mascarpone in a bowl until softened. Stir in the lemon juice and the melted chocolate mixture. *

3 Whip the cream until it holds its shape, then gently fold it into the mascarpone and chocolate mixture. Fold in the chopped chocolate chips. Turn into a freezer container, cover and freeze for at least 4 hours until firm.

4 To make the coffee syrup, heat the remaining sugar and the remaining water in a small heavy-based saucepan until the sugar dissolves. Bring to the boil and boil for 5 minutes until syrupy. Remove from the heat and stir in the coffee liqueur. Leave to cool, then chill until ready to serve.

5 Transfer the ice cream to the refrigerator about 30 minutes before serving to soften slightly. Stir the reserved chocolate chips into the syrup. Scoop the ice cream on to serving plates, spoon the coffee syrup over the ice cream and serve immediately.

* *If using an ice cream machine follow the recipe until the end of step **2**. Pour the mascarpone and chocolate mixture into the machine, add the cream and churn and freeze. Once frozen fold in the chopped chocolate chips. Resume the recipe at step **4**.*

Serves 6
Preparation time: **30 minutes, plus cooling and freezing**
Cooking time: **10–15 minutes**

walnut tuiles

50 g (2 oz) butter

2 egg whites

65 g (2½ oz) caster sugar

50 g (2 oz) plain flour, sifted

25 g (1 oz) walnut halves, coarsely chopped

a little icing sugar, sifted

After baking, these French biscuits are pressed gently into shape, to resemble a curved ridge tile. They will set hard in about 1 minute, so it is advisable to cook and shape only three or four at a time. Because they need to be cooked on cool baking sheets each time, it is a good idea to have three sheets in use.

1 Melt the butter gently over a low heat and leave to cool. Beat the egg whites in a bowl until frothy, then add the caster sugar and beat for about 2–3 minutes until the mixture thickens. Gently fold in the sifted flour, melted butter and chopped walnuts.

2 Lightly grease 3 baking sheets. Drop 3 or 4 small spoonfuls of the mixture on to a sheet. Spread each biscuit into a shallow circle. Dust with a little sifted icing sugar. Bake in a preheated oven, 200°C (400°F), Gas Mark 6, for about 5 minutes, or until golden brown around the edges.

3 Carefully remove the biscuits from the baking sheets and place on a lightly greased rolling pin, pressing gently with the hands to make the tile shape. When set, place on a wire rack and leave to go cold.

4 Cook the remaining biscuits in the same way, using a cool baking sheet for each batch.

Variation: Coarsely chopped hazelnuts or flaked almonds may be substituted for the walnuts.

Makes 20
Preparation time: **15 minutes**
Cooking time: **about 30 minutes**

chocolate chip ice cream

300 ml (½ pint) milk

75 g (3 oz) soft dark brown sugar

75 g (3 oz) plain chocolate, broken into pieces

2 eggs, beaten

½ teaspoon vanilla essence

300 ml (½ pint) double cream

75 g (3 oz) chocolate chips

mini chocolate cookies, to serve (optional)

1 Put the milk, sugar and chocolate into a saucepan and heat gently until the chocolate has melted and the sugar dissolved. Pour the warm mixture on to the beaten eggs, stirring constantly.

2 Return the mixture to the pan and cook over a low heat, stirring constantly, until the custard thickens very slightly. Strain the mixture into a bowl and add the vanilla essence. Leave to cool. *

3 Whip the cream until it forms soft peaks, then whisk it into the cooled custard.

4 Stir in the chocolate chips. Turn the mixture into a freezer container, cover and freeze until firm.

5 About 30 minutes before serving, transfer the ice cream to the refrigerator to soften. Spoon or scoop the ice cream into individual dishes and serve with mini chocolate cookies.

* *If using an ice cream machine follow the recipe until the end of step 2. Pour the mixture into the machine, add the cream and churn and freeze. Once frozen fold in the chocolate chips. Follow the serving suggestion at the end of step 5.*

Serves 4–6
Preparation time: **15 minutes, plus cooling and freezing**
Cooking time: **15 minutes**

chocolate maple ice cream

50 g (2 oz) raisins

4 tablespoons boiling water

2 egg yolks

50 g (2 oz) soft brown sugar

50 g (2 oz) plain chocolate, broken into pieces

3 tablespoons maple syrup

300 ml (½ pint) double cream, whipped

langues de chat or wafer biscuits, to serve

1 Place the raisins in a bowl and add the boiling water. Leave to soak for 15 minutes, then drain and set aside.

2 In a large bowl, whisk the egg yolks and sugar until thick and pale. Combine the chocolate and maple syrup in a heatproof bowl and place over a pan of gently simmering water. Stir until the chocolate has melted. Leave to cool,* then combine with the egg mixture and fold in the whipped cream. Mix well, then spoon into a freezer container, cover and freeze for 12 hours.

3 Spoon the ice cream into a bowl and beat until smooth, then fold in the raisins. Return to the rinsed container and freeze until firm.

4 Transfer the ice cream to the refrigerator 30 minutes before serving to soften slightly. Serve with langues de chat or wafer biscuits.

* *If using an ice cream machine follow the recipe until mid way through step 2. Place the egg mixture and chocolate mixture in the machine, add the cream and churn and freeze. Once frozen fold in the raisins. Follow the serving suggestion at the end of step 4.*

Serves 4–6
Preparation time: **20 minutes, plus cooling and freezing**

butterscotch sauce

50 g (2 oz) butter

50 g (2 oz) demerara sugar

50 g (2 oz) golden syrup

150 ml (¼ pint) milk

1 Put the butter, sugar and golden syrup into a heavy-based saucepan. Heat gently until the sugar has dissolved. Increase the heat and cook rapidly until the syrup reaches a temperature of 113–118°C/235–245°F on a sugar thermometer – soft ball stage (see page 10).

2 Remove the pan from the heat and leave to cool slightly, then slowly beat in the milk.

Makes about 300 ml (½ pint)
Preparation time: **10 minutes**
Cooking time: **about 10 minutes**

pecan praline ice cream

300 ml (½ pint) single cream

1 egg and 2 extra yolks

75 g (3 oz) caster sugar

300 ml (½ pint) double or

whipping cream

praline:

75 g (3 oz) caster sugar

75 g (3 oz) pecan halves

1 Heat the single cream in a small pan to just below boiling point. Then remove from the heat.

2 Put the egg, egg yolks and sugar into a heatproof bowl and whisk together. Stir in the hot cream and place the bowl over a pan of simmering water. Stir constantly with a wooden spoon for about 20 minutes until the custard is thick enough to coat the back of the spoon.* Strain into a freezer container, cover and freeze until slushy.

3 Meanwhile, make the praline. Place the sugar and pecans in a saucepan over a medium heat until the sugar caramelizes. Do not stir. Pour the mixture on to a buttered baking sheet and leave until cold. When cold, either grate in a rotary grater or grind in a coffee grinder.

4 Remove the egg custard from the freezer and beat until smooth. Whip the cream until it stands in soft peaks. Fold it into the custard with three-quarters of the praline. Return to the container and freeze until solid.

5 To serve, scoop spoonfuls of the ice cream into a serving dish and sprinkle with the remaining praline.

***** *If using an ice cream machine follow the recipe until mid way through step 2. Pour the cooled custard into the machine, add the cream and churn and freeze. Once frozen fold in three quarters of the praline. Follow the serving suggestion at the end of step 5.*

Serves 6
Preparation time: **45 minutes, plus freezing and cooling**
Cooking time: **25–30 minutes**

apricot & amaretto ice cream

250 g (8 oz) ready-to-eat
dried apricots

2 tablespoons Amaretto di Saronno

150 ml (¼ pint) double or
whipping cream

125 g (4 oz) granulated sugar

150 ml (¼ pint) water

2 egg whites

to serve:

warm toffee sauce (see below)

amaretti biscuits (optional)

1 Place the apricots in a saucepan and cover with cold water. Cover the pan and simmer gently for 15 minutes or until soft.

2 Drain the apricots, transfer to a food processor or blender and process to a purée. Leave to cool, then transfer to a medium bowl and stir in the liqueur. Whip the cream until it forms soft peaks, then gently fold it into the apricot purée.

3 Place the sugar and water in a heavy-based pan and heat gently until the sugar dissolves, stirring all the time, then boil, until the syrup registers 120°C/248°F on a sugar thermometer – hard ball stage (see page 10).

4 Meanwhile, put the egg whites into a bowl and beat until stiff. Slowly pour on the boiling syrup, beating the egg whites at high speed all the time and continuing to beat until cool.

5 Combine the apricot mixture and the egg white mixture together, mixing well. Transfer the mixture to a freezer container, cover and freeze until firm. without further beating. Serve with amaretti biscuits and hot fudge sauce if liked.

* *Please note that there is no need to make this ice cream in an ice cream machine.*

Serves 4
Preparation time: **20 minutes, plus
   cooling and freezing**
Cooking time: **25 minutes**

warm toffee sauce

75 g (3 oz) butter

1 tablespoon golden syrup

75 g (3 oz) brown sugar

4 tablespoons evaporated milk

1 Place all the ingredients in a heavy-based saucepan and heat gently, stirring constantly with a wooden spoon, until the sugar has dissolved.

2 Bring to the boil, then remove the pan from the heat. Serve warm.

Serves 4–6
Preparation time: **5 minutes**
Cooking time: **10 minutes**

honeyed banana ice cream with nuts

500 g (1 lb) bananas, peeled

2 tablespoons lemon juice

3 tablespoons thick honey

150 ml (¼ pint) natural yogurt

50 g (2 oz) chopped nuts

150 ml (¼ pint) double cream

2 egg whites

pralines (see page 11), to serve

1 Put the bananas into a bowl with the lemon juice and mash until smooth. Stir in the honey, then the yogurt and nuts and beat well.

2 Whip the cream until it forms soft peaks and fold into the banana mixture. * Transfer the mixture to a freezer container, cover and freeze until partially set.

3 Whisk the egg whites until stiff. Beat the banana mixture to break up the ice crystals, then fold in the egg whites and freeze until firm. Serve with pralines if liked.

** If using an ice cream machine follow the recipe until mid way through step **2**. Transfer the banana mixture to the ice cream machine and churn and freeze until half frozen. Whisk the egg whites until they form soft peaks, then add to the half-frozen mixture. Continue to freeze until completely frozen. Follow the serving suggestion at end of step **3**.*

Serves 4–6
Preparation time: **15 minutes,
    plus freezing**

chocolate truffle & coffee
ice cream

125 g (4 oz) plain chocolate, finely chopped

2 tablespoons single cream

2 tablespoons rum

coffee ice cream:

2 tablespoons instant coffee granules

2 tablespoons boiling water

2 egg whites

125 g (4 oz) caster sugar

300 ml (½ pint) double cream

walnut tuiles (see page 32), to serve (optional)

1 Place the chocolate, cream and rum in a heatproof bowl over a pan of simmering water and leave until the chocolate has melted. Mix well, then set aside to cool.

2 To make the ice cream, dissolve the coffee granules in the boiling water and leave to cool. Whisk the egg whites until stiff, then whisk in the sugar. Whip the cream with the coffee until it forms soft peaks. Fold the coffee cream into the meringue mixture.

3 When the chocolate truffle mixture begins to thicken, stir it until it is smooth and soft, then fold it into the ice cream mixture very lightly to create a marbled effect. Turn the mixture into a freezer container, cover and freeze until firm.

4 Transfer the ice cream to the refrigerator 30 minutes before serving, to soften slightly. Scoop into chilled sundae glasses and serve with walnut tuiles if liked.

* *Please note that this ice cream cannot be made in an ice cream machine.*

Serves 8
Preparation time: **15 minutes, plus cooling and freezing**
Cooking time: **10 minutes**

cinnamon pear ice cream

500 g (1 lb) ripe pears, peeled, cored and chopped

2 tablespoons lemon juice

2 tablespoons golden syrup

50 g (2 oz) butter

1 teaspoon ground cinnamon

1 egg and 1 extra egg yolk

150 ml (¼ pint) double or whipping cream

mint leaves, to decorate

1 Place the pears in a saucepan with the lemon juice, golden syrup, butter and cinnamon. Bring slowly to the boil, then simmer uncovered until the pears are soft. Purée the pears in a food processor or blender, then return the purée to the rinsed pan.

2 Put the egg and the extra yolk into a bowl and beat together. Stir the beaten eggs into the pear mixture, then place the pan over a very gentle heat and continue to stir until the mixture thickens. Set aside to cool. *

3 Transfer the pear mixture to a freezer container. Whip the cream until it forms soft peaks and fold it into the pear mixture. Cover and freeze until firm, beating twice at hourly intervals. Serve in individual dishes and decorate with mint leaves.

* *If using an ice cream machine follow the recipe until the end of step **2**. Pour the pear mixture into the machine, add the cream and churn and freeze. Follow the serving suggestion at the end of step **3**.*

Serves 4–6
Preparation time: **20 minutes, plus cooling and freezing**
Cooking time: **20 minutes**

peppermint candy ice cream

50 g (2 oz) peppermint candy canes
or peppermint rock

4 egg yolks

50 g (2 oz) caster sugar

1 teaspoon cornflour

300 ml (½ pint) milk

300 ml (½ pint) whipping cream

extra crushed peppermint candy
or peppermint rock, to
decorate (optional)

1 Put the candy canes or rock into a polythene bag and beat with the end of a rolling pin until roughly crushed. Continue to beat until the candy is broken into small granules.

2 Beat the egg yolks in a bowl with the sugar, cornflour and a little of the milk until smooth. Bring the remaining milk to the boil in a heavy-based saucepan. Pour the milk over the egg yolk mixture, whisking well until combined. Return the mixture to the saucepan and cook very gently, stirring until it has thickened enough to coat the back of the spoon thinly.

3 Transfer the custard to a bowl, cover with a circle of greaseproof paper to prevent a skin from forming and leave to cool. Chill in the refrigerator until very cold. *

4 Lightly whip the cream and fold it into the custard with the crushed candy. Turn into a freezer container, cover and freeze until the mixture has frozen around the edges. Transfer to a bowl and whisk lightly.

5 Return to the freezer until the mixture has once again frozen around the edges. Repeat the whisking and freezing once or twice more, then freeze the ice cream until ready to serve.

6 Transfer the ice cream to the refrigerator about 30 minutes before serving to soften slightly. Scoop into glasses and sprinkle with extra crushed peppermint candy, if you like.

* *If using an ice cream machine follow the recipe until the end of step 3. Transfer the custard to the machine, add the cream and churn and freeze. Follow the serving suggestion at the end of step 6.*

Serves 4
Preparation time: **20 minutes,
    plus freezing**
Cooking time: **5 minutes**

lavender honey ice cream with roasted figs

6 tablespoons lavender honey

4 egg yolks

1 teaspoon cornflour

1 tablespoon caster sugar

300 ml (½ pint) milk

300 ml (½ pint) whipping cream

lavender sprigs, to
decorate (optional)

roasted figs:

4 large fresh figs

2 tablespoons clear honey

1 tablespoon fresh orange juice

If you can't get lavender-flavoured honey, use another mild flower honey and add the flowers of eight lavender sprigs to the custard.

1 Put the honey, egg yolks, cornflour and sugar into a bowl and whisk lightly to combine. Bring the milk to the boil in a heavy-based saucepan. Pour the milk over the egg yolk mixture, whisking well until combined. Return the mixture to the saucepan and cook very gently, stirring constantly, until the custard has thickened enough to coat the back of the spoon thinly. Transfer to a bowl and cover with a circle of greaseproof paper to prevent a skin from forming. Leave to cool, then chill in the refrigerator until very cold. *

2 Lightly whip the cream and gently fold it into the custard. Turn the mixture into a freezer container, cover and freeze until it has frozen around the edges. Transfer to a bowl and whisk lightly. Re-freeze until the mixture has once again frozen around the edges. Repeat the whisking and freezing once or twice more.

3 Meanwhile, to cook the figs, cut a cross in the top of each one and place in a shallow ovenproof dish. Brush the figs with the honey and drizzle with the orange juice. Roast in a preheated oven, 220°C (425°F), Gas Mark 7, for about 10 minutes until lightly caramelized around the edges.

4 To serve, transfer the ice cream to the refrigerator 30 minutes before serving, to soften slightly. Scoop into serving glasses with the figs, spooning over any juices. Decorate with lavender sprigs if you like.

* *If using an ice cream machine follow the recipe until the end of step 1. Pour the mixture into the machine, add the cream and churn and freeze. Follow the serving suggestion at the end of step 4.*

Serves 4
Preparation time: **20 minutes, plus chilling and freezing**
Cooking time: **15 minutes**

summer berry sorbet

250 g (8 oz) frozen mixed summer berries

75 ml (3 fl oz) spiced berry cordial

2 tablespoons Kirsch or vodka

1 tablespoon fresh lime juice

As an alternative you could make three types of berry sorbet and serve them together.

1 Chill a shallow freezer container. Put the berries, cordial, Kirsch or vodka, and lime juice into a food processor or blender and purée until smooth. Do not over-process, as this will soften the mixture too much.

2 Turn the purée into the chilled container, cover and freeze for at least 25 minutes. Spoon the sorbet into bowls and serve.

* *Please note that there is no need to make this sorbet in an ice cream machine.*

Serves 2
Preparation time: **5 minutes, plus freezing**

plum sorbet

750 g (1½ lb) Victoria plums, halved and pitted

250 g (8 oz) caster sugar

600 ml (1 pint) water

1 cinnamon stick

strip of lemon rind

to decorate:

1 plum, cut into 4 slices

mint sprigs

1 Place the plums in a roasting tin and cook in a preheated oven, 200°C/400°F, Gas Mark 6, for 45 minutes.

2 Put the sugar, water, cinnamon stick and lemon rind into a saucepan. Dissolve the sugar over a low heat and bring to the boil. Cook over a medium heat for 20 minutes until syrupy.

3 Transfer the cooked plums to the sugar syrup and cook for 10 minutes. Remove from the heat and discard the lemon rind and cinnamon stick.

4 Purée the fruit mixture in a food processor or blender. * Leave to cool, then freeze for 3 hours until just frozen.

Remove the sorbet from the freezer and mash with a fork, then return to the freezer for a further 3 hours.

5 Remove from the freezer 10 minutes before you are ready to serve. Scoop into glasses and decorate with plum slices and mint sprigs.

* *If using an ice cream machine follow the recipe until mid way through step 4. Pour the mixture into the machine and churn and freeze. Decorate with plum slices and mint sprigs.*

Serves 4
Preparation time: **10 minutes, plus cooling and freezing**
Cooking time: **55 minutes**

tangerine sorbet

10 tangerines

175 g (6 oz) caster sugar

6 tablespoons water

juice of 2 lemons

mint sprigs, to decorate

orange flavoured liqueur, to serve (optional)

This refreshing sorbet is the perfect dessert after a rich main course or as a cooling treat on a hot summer's afternoon.

1 Peel the tangerines. Cut the segments in half and discard the seeds. Purée the flesh in a food processor or blender, then press through a sieve to extract as much juice as possible. Transfer the juice to a measuring jug.

2 Put the sugar and water into a heavy-based saucepan and heat until the sugar has dissolved. Bring to the boil and boil for 3 minutes until syrupy.

3 Add the syrup to the tangerine juice with the lemon juice. You will need about 900 ml (1½ pints) of liquid. Make up with extra tangerine juice or fresh orange juice, if necessary.*

4 Pour the tangerine syrup into a freezer container, cover and freeze for about 2 hours or until a thick layer of ice crystals has formed around the edges. Transfer the sorbet to a bowl and whisk lightly.

5 Return to the freezer until the mixture has once again frozen around the edges. Repeat the whisking and freezing until the sorbet is thick and smooth, then freeze until ready to serve.

6 Transfer the sorbet to the refrigerator about 45 minutes before serving to soften slightly. Pile into glasses, decorate with mint sprigs and drizzle with a little orange liqueur if you like.

* *If using an ice cream machine follow the recipe to the end of step 3. Pour the mixture into the machine and churn and freeze. Follow the serving suggestion at the end of step 6.*

Serves 6
Preparation time: **10 minutes, plus freezing**
Cooking time: **3 minutes**

fresh pineapple water ice

450 ml (¾ pint) water

150 g (5 oz) granulated sugar

1 strip of lemon rind

1 fresh ripe pineapple, weighing about 1.25 kg (2½ lb)

2 teaspoons gelatine

1 Put the water, sugar and lemon rind into a heavy saucepan and heat gently until the sugar has dissolved. Bring to the boil, then boil for 5 minutes until syrupy. Remove from the heat, leave to cool, then remove and discard the lemon rind.

2 Meanwhile, cut the pineapple in half lengthways and scoop out the flesh. Reserve the shells, wrap them closely in foil and chill in the refrigerator until serving time. Purée the flesh in a food processor or blender and measure out 450 ml (¾ pint).

3 Pour 150 ml (¼ pint) of the cooled syrup into a small bowl and sprinkle over the gelatine. Stir to dissolve, then leave for 5 minutes. Stand the bowl in a pan of simmering water and heat gently until dissolved. Stir the dissolved gelatine into the remaining syrup, then leave until completely cold.

4 *Combine the syrup and the pineapple purée, then pour into a freezer container and chill in the refrigerator for at least 30 minutes. Transfer to the freezer and freeze for 1–2 hours or until slushy.

5 Remove the mixture from the freezer and beat thoroughly. Cover and re-freeze for at least 2 hours or until firm.

6 Stand the water ice at room temperature for 10–20 minutes to soften slightly, then scoop into the chilled pineapple shells. Serve immediately.

***** *If using an ice cream machine follow the recipe until the beginning of step **4**. Pour the syrup and pineapple purée into the machine and churn and freeze. Follow the serving suggestion at the end of step **6**.*

Serves 4–6
Preparation time: **30 minutes, plus cooling and freezing**
Cooking time: **10 minutes**

apricot & orange sorbet

150 g (5 oz) caster sugar

300 ml (½ pint) water

75 ml (3 fl oz) fresh orange juice

3 tablespoons fresh lemon juice

grated rind of 1 orange

500 g (1 lb) ripe apricots, halved and pitted

1 egg white

sugared mint strips, to decorate (optional)

1 Put the sugar, water, orange and lemon juices and orange rind into a saucepan and bring to the boil, stirring until the sugar has dissolved. Increase the heat and boil rapidly for about 5 minutes until the syrup registers 107°C/225°F on a sugar thermometer – thread stage (see page 10). Add the apricots and simmer gently for about 2 minutes until they have softened slightly. Leave them to cool in the syrup.

2 Pour the fruit and syrup into a food processor or blender and process to a smooth purée.* Pour into a freezer container, cover and freeze for about 2 hours until frozen around the sides but slushy in the centre.

3 Tip the frozen syrup into a bowl and whisk briefly until smooth. Whisk the egg white until it forms soft peaks and fold into the fruit using a metal spoon. Pour the mixture back into the container and freeze for about 6 hours.

4 Transfer the sorbet to the refrigerator about 20 minutes before serving to soften slightly. To serve, arrange scoops of sorbet in individual glasses and decorate with sugared mint strips, if liked.

* *If using an ice cream machine follow the recipe until mid way through step 2. Then pour into the machine and freeze until half-frozen. Whisk the egg whites until they form soft peaks and add to the half-frozen mixture. Continue to freeze until completely frozen. Follow the serving suggestion at the end of step 4.*

Serves 6–8
Preparation time: **20 minutes, plus cooling and freezing**
Cooking time: **8 minutes**

fresh melon sorbet

1 canteloupe melon, weighing
1 kg (2 lb)

50 g (2 oz) icing sugar

juice of 1 lime or small lemon

1 egg white

Other flavoursome melons, such as honeydew or watermelon, may be used for this sorbet. For a dinner party, make three sorbets using different types of melon: the different coloured flesh and subtly different flavours make a very special dessert.

1 Cut the melon in half and scoop out and discard the seeds. Scoop out the melon flesh with a spoon and discard the shells.

2 Place the flesh in a food processor or blender with the icing sugar and lime or lemon juice. Process to a purée,* then pour into a freezer container, cover and freeze for 2–3 hours.

3 Whisk the melon mixture to break up the ice crystals. Whisk the egg white until stiff, then whisk it into the half-frozen melon mixture. Return to the freezer until firm.

4 Transfer the sorbet to the refrigerator 20 minutes before serving to soften slightly. Scoop the sorbet into glass dishes to serve.

* *If using an ice cream machine follow the recipe until mid way through step 2. Pour into the machine and churn and freeze until half-frozen. Whisk the egg whites until they form soft peaks and add to the machine. Continue to freeze until completely frozen.*

Serves 4–6
Preparation time: **15 minutes,
    plus freezing**

tangy lemon sorbet

600 ml (1 pint) water

250 g (8 oz) granulated sugar

3 tablespoons water

3 teaspoons gelatine

rind of 2 lemons

300 ml (½ pint) fresh lemon juice

2 egg whites

candied lemon peel (see page 11),
to serve (optional)

1 Put the water and sugar into a small pan and heat gently until the sugar dissolves. Bring to the boil and boil steadily for 10 minutes. Leave to cool.

2 Put the water in a small bowl and sprinkle on the gelatine. Set the bowl over a pan of simmering water and leave until the gelatine goes spongy. Whisk the gelatine mixture into the syrup with the lemon rind and juice.*

3 Pour the lemon mixture into a freezer container, cover and freeze for about 1 hour until partially frozen. Turn the partially frozen mixture into a chilled bowl and beat lightly to break up the crystals.

4 Whisk the egg whites until stiff and carefully fold into the lemon mixture. Freeze for a further 1½ hours, then whisk again and freeze until firm. Decorate with candied lemon peel.

* If using an ice cream machine follow the recipe until the end of step 2. Pour the mixture into the machine and churn and freeze until half-frozen. Whisk the egg whites until they form soft peaks and add to the half-frozen mixture. Freeze again until completely frozen. Decorate with candied lemon peel.

Serves 4–6
Preparation time: **15 minutes, plus cooling and freezing**
Cooking time: **10–15 minutes**

pear sorbet

500 g (1 lb) ripe dessert pears, peeled, cored and sliced

2 tablespoons lemon juice

2 tablespoons clear honey

2 egg whites

1 Place the pears, lemon juice and honey in a medium saucepan. Cover and simmer until the fruit is soft.

2 Purée the pears in a food processor or blender and leave to cool.* Spoon into a container and freeze for about 1½ hours until slushy.

3 Beat the egg whites until stiff. Remove the pear mixture from the freezer and beat to break up the ice crystals. Gently fold in the egg whites and freeze until firm.

* If using an ice cream machine follow the recipe until mid way through step 2. Pour the mixture into the machine and churn and freeze until half-frozen. Whisk the egg whites until they form soft peaks and add to the half-frozen mixture. Continue to freeze until completely frozen.

Serves 4
Preparation time: **15 minutes, plus cooling and freezing**
Cooking time: **10 minutes**

blood orange granita

1 kg (2 lb) blood oranges

250 g (8 oz) sugar

1 Using a sharp knife, cut off the tops and bottoms of the oranges, then cut away the pith and peel. Working over a bowl to catch the juice, cut the segments out of the oranges and squeeze any excess juice from them.

2 Strain the juice into a saucepan, add the sugar and heat gently until it has completely dissolved.

3 Place the orange flesh in a food processor or blender and process until smooth. Stir in the juice, then pour into ice cube trays and freeze until firm.

4 Chill the serving glasses for a short while in the freezer before serving. To serve, remove the granita cubes from the freezer, put them in the food processor or blender and process for 30 seconds, then transfer the ice to the chilled glasses and serve immediately.

* *Please note that granitas should not be made in an ice cream machine.*

Serves 4
Preparation time: **10 minutes, plus freezing**

orange and passion fruit granita

575 ml (18 fl oz) orange juice

2 passion fruit

4–6 teaspoons grenadine

1 Pour the orange juice into a freezer container. Cut the passion fruit in half and squeeze out the pulp. Stir into the juice and freeze until almost hard.

2 Tip the frozen juice into a roasting tin and, using a metal fork, break it up into small pieces. Spoon the crystals into a freezer bag, fasten and return to the freezer until required.

3 To serve, first chill 4–6 tall glasses in the refrigerator for 15–20 minutes, then spoon some of the frozen crystals into each glass and top each portion with 1 teaspoon of grenadine.

* *Please note that granitas should not be made in an ice cream machine.*

Serves 4–6
Preparation time: **10 minutes, plus freezing**

lemon honey granita

4 large or 6 medium lemons

about 4 tablespoons water

2 tablespoons clear honey

50 g (2 oz) caster sugar

1 fresh bay leaf or 1 lemon balm sprig

450 ml (¾ pint) natural yogurt or fromage frais

lemon balm sprigs, to decorate

1 Cut a slice from the base of each lemon so that it will stand upright without wobbling.

2 Slice off the top of each lemon and reserve. Carefully scoop out all the pulp and juice with a teaspoon; do this over a bowl, so that no juice is wasted. Discard any white pith, skin and pips from the flesh you have removed. Sieve or blend the pulp and juice. You need 150 ml (¼ pint). If there is less than this, dilute it with water. Cut out any excess pith from the lemon shells and from the reserved tops.

3 Put the water into a saucepan with the honey, sugar and bay leaf or lemon balm. Stir over a low heat until the sugar has dissolved, then leave to cool. Mix with the lemon purée and the yogurt or fromage frais. Do not remove the herb at this stage.

4 Pour into a shallow freezer container, cover and place in the freezer until lightly frozen, then gently fork the mixture and remove the herb. Re-freeze the granita for a short time, until it is sufficiently firm to spoon into the lemon shells. Replace the tops of the lemons and place the fruit in the freezer.

5 Transfer the granitas to the refrigerator about 20 minutes before serving. Serve decorated with lemon balm sprigs.

Variation: Use 4–6 oranges instead of lemons. Honey is less good with oranges, so omit it and use just the sugar. Use a mixture of half orange purée and half yogurt or fromage frais.

* *Please note that granitas should not be made in an ice cream machine.*

Serves 4–6
Preparation time: **20 minutes, plus cooling and freezing**

coffee granita

4 tablespoons freshly ground strong coffee

125 g (4 oz) caster sugar

450 ml (¾ pint) boiling water

whipped cream, to serve (optional)

1 Put the ground coffee and sugar into a jug and stir in the boiling water. Stir until the sugar has dissolved, then leave to cool.

2 Strain the coffee liquid into a freezer container, cover and chill in the refrigerator for about 30 minutes. Transfer to the freezer and freeze for at least 2 hours or until completely solid.

3 Remove the granita from the container, then quickly chop it into large chunks with a large strong knife. Return it to the container and freeze again until required. Serve straight from the freezer, with whipped cream if you like.

* *Please note that granitas should not be made in an ice cream machine.*

Serves 4
Preparation time: **10 minutes, plus cooling and freezing**

Campari granita

75 g (3 oz) caster sugar

150 ml (¼ pint) water

450 ml (¾ pint) fresh orange juice

175 ml (6 fl oz) Campari

1 Heat the sugar and water in a saucepan until the sugar has dissolved, then bring to the boil and boil for 3 minutes. Leave to cool.

2 Mix the syrup with the orange juice and Campari and pour into a shallow freezer container. Cover and freeze for about 2 hours until a thick layer of ice crystals has formed around the edges.

3 Using a fork, break up the ice crystals, stirring them into the centre of the container. Return to the freezer for a further 30 minutes or until more ice crystals have formed around the edges.

4 Repeat the forking and freezing until the mixture has the consistency of crushed ice. Freeze until ready to serve.

5 To serve, lightly stir the granita with a fork and pile it into tall glasses.

* *Please note that granitas should not be made in an ice cream machine.*

Serves 4
Preparation time: **15 minutes, plus freezing**
Cooking time: **5 minutes**

Champagne water ice

250 g (8 oz) sugar

300 ml (½ pint) water

300 ml (½ pint) Champagne

juice of 1 lemon and 1 orange

strawberries, to serve

1 Put the sugar and water into a heavy-based saucepan and heat until the sugar has dissolved.

2 Stir the Champagne and fruit juices into the sugar syrup, * then pour into a shallow container and freeze. When the mixture is frozen around the edges, but still soft in the centre, tip it into a food processor and process until smooth. Return it to the container and re-freeze.

3 Repeat the whisking at intervals until the ice is creamy, smooth and white. Serve with strawberries.

* *If using an ice cream machine follow the recipe until mid way through step 2. Then pour the mixture into the machine and churn and freeze. Serve with strawberries.*

Serves 6
Preparation time: **15 minutes, plus cooling and freezing**
Cooking time: **5–10 minutes**

citrus and rum sorbet

1½ teaspoons gelatine

125 ml (4 fl oz) cold water

75 g (3 oz) caster sugar

1 tablespoon fresh lime juice

50 ml (2 fl oz) white rum

125 ml (4 fl oz) fresh orange juice

to decorate:

fresh mint leaves,

fine strips of candied orange peel

1 Sprinkle the gelatine over 2 tablespoons of the water in a small heatproof bowl. Leave until spongy, then stand the bowl in a pan of simmering water. Heat gently, stirring, until the gelatine has dissolved, then remove the bowl from the heat.

2 Bring the sugar and the remaining water to the boil in a small, heavy-based saucepan and simmer for 1 minute. Stir in the dissolved gelatine. Add the lime juice, rum, orange juice and rind and cook for 30 seconds over a low heat. Remove from the heat and leave to cool. *

3 Strain the mixture into a shallow freezer container, cover and freeze until slushy. Then tip the mixture into a bowl and beat until smooth. Return to the container and freeze until almost solid. Scoop into glasses and decorate with mint or candied orange peel.

* *If using an ice cream machine follow the recipe until the end of step 2. Pour the mixture into the machine and churn and freeze. Follow the serving suggestion at the end of step 3.*

Serves 4
Preparation time: **15 minutes, plus cooling and freezing**
Cooking time: **5 minutes**

Index

a

almonds:
  cherry almond ice cream **20**
  pralines **11**
apricots:
  apricot and amaretto ice
   cream **38**
  apricot and orange sorbet **52**

b

baked Alaska **10**
bananas:
  banana split **10**
  honeyed banana ice cream **40**
biscuits:
  walnut tuiles **32**
blackberry ice cream **12**
blood orange granita **58**
boiling sugar **10**
bombes **10**
butterscotch sauce **36**

c

Campari granita **60**
caramel **10**
  caramelized cherries **11**
  hot caramel sauce **22**
Champagne water ice **62**
charlottes **10**
cherries:
  caramelized cherries **11**
  cherry almond ice cream **20**
  cherry chocolate ice cream **19**
chocolate:
  cherry chocolate ice cream **19**
  chocolate and mascarpone
   ice cream **31**
  chocolate chip ice cream **34**
  chocolate ice cream **28**
  chocolate maple ice cream **36**
  chocolate sauce **28**

  chocolate truffle and coffee

   ice cream **42**
  mint chocolate chip ice
   cream **30**
  rocky road ice cream **24**
cinnamon pear ice cream **43**
citrus and rum sorbet **62**
coconut ice cream **25**
coffee:
  chocolate truffle and coffee
   ice cream **42**
  coffee granita **60**
cream ices **10**

d

decorations **11**

f

figs, roasted **46**
fudge sauce **30**

g

ginger:
  crystallized ginger ice cream **16**
granitas **10**
  blood orange **58**
  Campari **60**
  coffee **60**
  lemon honey **59**
  orange and passion fruit **58**
greengage plum ice cream **26**

h

honey:
  honeyed banana ice cream **40**
  lavender honey ice cream **46**
  lemon honey granita **59**

l

lavender honey ice cream **46**
lemon:
  lemon honey granita **59**
  tangy lemon sorbet **56**

m

mango ice cream **14**
melon sorbet **54**
mint chocolate chip ice cream **30**

o

orange:
  apricot and orange sorbet **52**
  blood orange granita **58**
  Campari granita **60**
  orange and passion fruit
   granita **58**

p

peaches:
  peach ice cream **16**
  peach Melba **10**
pears:
  cinnamon pear ice cream **43**
  pear sorbet **56**
pecan praline ice cream **37**
peppermint candy ice cream **44**
pineapple water ice **51**
plum sorbet **48**
pralines **11**

r

raspberries:
  peach Melba **10**
rocky road ice cream **24**
rum:
  citrus and rum sorbet **62**
  rum and raisin ice cream **18**

s

sauces:
  butterscotch **32**
  chocolate **28**
  hot fudge **30**
  hot caramel **22**
  warm toffee **38**
sorbets **10**
  apricot and orange **52**

citrus and rum **62**
melon **54**
pear **56**
plum **48**
summer berry **48**
tangerine **50**
tangy lemon **56**
st clements ice cream **15**
storing ices **11**
strawberry ice cream **12**
sugar syrups **10**
summer berry sorbet **48**

t

tangerine sorbet **50**
tuiles, walnut **15**

v

vanilla ice cream, old-fashioned
22

w

walnut tuiles **32**
water ices **10**
  Champagne **62**
  pineapple **51**

Acknowledgements

Editor: Abi Rowsell
Copy Editor: Anne Crane
Designer: Claire Harvey
Production Controller: Jo Sim

Photographer: Stephen Conroy
Food Stylist: David Morgan
Stylist: Clare Hunt